First World War
and Army of Occupation
War Diary
France, Belgium and Germany

41 DIVISION
123 Infantry Brigade
Duke of Cambridge's Own (Middlesex Regiment)
23rd Battalion
1 March 1918 - 28 February 1919

WO95/2639/3

The Naval & Military Press Ltd
www.nmarchive.com
Published in association with The National Archives

Published by

The Naval & Military Press Ltd

Unit 10 Ridgewood Industrial Park,
Uckfield, East Sussex,
TN22 5QE England
Tel: +44 (0) 1825 749494

www.naval-military-press.com

www.nmarchive.com

This diary has been reprinted in facsimile from the original. Any imperfections are inevitably reproduced and the quality may fall short of modern type and cartographic standards.

© **Crown Copyright**
Images reproduced by permission of The National Archives, London, England, 2015.

Contents

Document type	Place/Title	Date From	Date To
Heading	WO95/2639/3		
Heading	23rd Battn. The Middlesex Regiment. March 1918		
War Diary	Moline	01/03/1918	03/03/1918
War Diary	Camp Demarte	03/03/1918	03/03/1918
War Diary	Bologna	03/03/1918	03/03/1918
War Diary	Train A V. 17	03/03/1918	09/03/1918
War Diary	Coullemont	10/03/1918	21/03/1918
War Diary	Bouzincourt	21/03/1918	22/03/1918
War Diary	Beugny	22/03/1918	23/03/1918
War Diary	Favreiul	24/03/1918	24/03/1918
War Diary	Monument	25/03/1918	25/03/1918
War Diary	Beinvillers	26/03/1918	27/03/1918
War Diary	Ablainzaville	28/03/1918	31/03/1918
Heading	23rd Battalion The Middlesex Regiment April 1918		
War Diary	Ablainzaville	01/04/1918	02/04/1918
War Diary	Bienvilliers	03/04/1918	03/04/1918
War Diary	Bonniere	04/04/1918	04/04/1918
War Diary	Eecke	05/04/1918	08/04/1918
War Diary	Junction Camp	09/04/1918	09/04/1918
War Diary	Front Line	10/04/1918	12/04/1918
War Diary	Plum Keep	13/04/1918	14/04/1918
War Diary	Wieltje	15/04/1918	26/04/1918
War Diary	V. 3	27/04/1918	30/04/1918
War Diary	Reserve Area V4 I 6 d	01/05/1918	03/05/1918
War Diary	Outpost Line	04/05/1918	10/05/1918
War Diary	Warrington Camp	11/05/1918	11/05/1918
War Diary	Orrilla Camp H. 2 W	12/05/1918	17/05/1918
War Diary	Ypres Defences	18/05/1918	21/05/1918
War Diary	Front Line	22/05/1918	30/05/1918
War Diary	Ypres Defences	30/05/1918	31/05/1918
War Diary	Ypres	01/06/1918	03/06/1918
War Diary	St. Janter Biesen	04/06/1918	05/06/1918
War Diary	St Momelin	05/06/1918	10/06/1918
War Diary	St Martin-Au-Laert	11/06/1918	25/06/1918
War Diary	Nieurlet	26/06/1918	26/06/1918
War Diary	Zermezeele	27/06/1918	30/06/1918
War Diary	Wippenhoek To Kemmel	01/07/1918	02/07/1918
War Diary	Kemmel	02/07/1918	06/07/1918
War Diary	Kasteel-Mill	06/07/1918	11/07/1918
War Diary	Laclytte	11/07/1918	16/07/1918
War Diary	Kemmel	16/07/1918	22/07/1918
War Diary	Wippenhoek Area	22/07/1918	30/07/1918
War Diary	Sheet 27 L. 30.a 90.05	01/08/1918	01/08/1918
War Diary	Dallington Camp	02/08/1918	02/08/1918
War Diary	Kemmel	02/08/1918	11/08/1918
War Diary	Loye	11/08/1918	18/08/1918
War Diary	Kemmel	18/08/1918	26/08/1918
War Diary	North Of Laclytte	26/08/1918	27/08/1918
War Diary	N. Of La Clytte	26/08/1918	30/08/1918
War Diary	St Martin	31/08/1918	31/08/1918

War Diary	St Martin-Au-Laert	01/09/1918	02/09/1918
War Diary	Ouderdom	03/09/1918	18/09/1918
War Diary	Wippenhoek	19/09/1918	30/09/1918
Miscellaneous	Headquarters. 123rd Inf. Brigade.	29/09/1918	29/09/1918
War Diary		01/10/1918	31/10/1918
Miscellaneous	H.Q. 123rd Brigade.	01/10/1918	01/10/1918
Miscellaneous	Headquarters, 123rd Infantry Brigade.	25/10/1918	25/10/1918
Miscellaneous	Headquarters, 123rd Infantry Brigade.	16/11/1918	16/11/1918
Heading	WO95/2639		
Map			
Heading	WO95/2639		
Map			
Heading	WO95/2639		
Miscellaneous			
War Diary	Courtran	01/11/1918	01/11/1918
War Diary	Sweveghem	02/11/1918	04/11/1918
War Diary	Kleinberg	05/11/1918	11/11/1918
War Diary	Hoogstraat	12/11/1918	13/11/1918
War Diary	Grammont	17/11/1918	18/11/1918
War Diary	Thellenbeck	19/11/1918	20/11/1918
War Diary	Ghoy	20/11/1918	12/12/1918
War Diary	Sopierne Capelle	13/12/1918	13/12/1918
War Diary	Lemberq Area	14/12/1918	16/12/1918
War Diary	Baesythy Area	17/12/1918	17/12/1918
War Diary	Sombreffe Area	18/12/1918	18/12/1918
War Diary	Carroy-Le-Chateau	19/12/1918	19/12/1918
War Diary	St Geman Village	20/12/1918	20/12/1918
War Diary	Ciplet	21/12/1918	21/12/1918
War Diary	Latinne	22/12/1918	31/12/1918
Heading	23rd Bn Middlesex Regt. Jan-Feb 1919		
Miscellaneous	Intelligence Officer 123rd Infantry Bde.	05/02/1919	05/02/1919
War Diary	Latinne	01/01/1919	10/01/1919
War Diary	Lynde	11/01/1919	16/01/1919
War Diary	Linds	17/01/1919	25/01/1919
War Diary	Lohmar	26/01/1919	31/01/1919
War Diary	Coln Kalk	01/02/1919	16/02/1919
Miscellaneous	123rd Infantry Bde.	03/03/1919	03/03/1919
War Diary	Coln-Kalk	17/02/1919	28/02/1919
Miscellaneous	Record of the 23rd. (S) Battn. Middlesex Regiment.		

Moss (1659)

123rd Inf.Bde.
41st Div.

Battn. with Bde. returned to France from Italy 2/8.3.18.

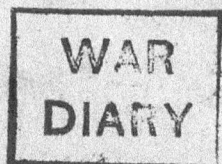

23rd BATTN. THE MIDDLESEX REGIMENT.

M A R C H

1 9 1 8

WAR DIARY or INTELLIGENCE SUMMARY

23rd Middlesex Regt. — March 1918 — Vol 2

Place	Date	Hour	Summary of Events and Information	Remarks and references to Appendices
Moline	March 1918 1	11 a.m.	Inspection of all companies on marching order by C.O.	
			Remainder of day devoted to rest.	
			Church Parade held by Capt. Foster C.F.	
			Party proceeds to Camps ahead to reconnoitre entraining scenery	
			3 K. west of Padova.	
	2	1/2 pm	Lorries leave Moline with first half Battalion for entraining	
			OC train Major Poole DSO, 13 officers & 489 OR. not to transport.	
			1st train leave Campo di Marte at 11 pm	
	3	6.15 am	2nd half Battalion entraining. Waiting for lorries these did not	
			arrive until 8.15 am. After considerable delay occasioned by	
			lorries breaking down the entraining was reached at 5 pm and	
			17 officers 466 OR 2nd half transport and 123 L/R evacuated sick	
Campo di Marte		11.15 am	3rd train under charge of C.O. leaves Campo di Marte	
			Accommodation for men was very tramped.	
			Owing to failure of lorries train left 3 hours late — one hour	
Bologna		5 pm	First meal halt — one hour.	

WAR DIARY or INTELLIGENCE SUMMARY

23rd Middlesex Regt.   Army Form C. 2118.

(Erase heading not required.)

Place	Date 1918	Hour	Summary of Events and Information	Remarks and references to Appendices
Train in Italy & France	Feb. 3		Parma 16.18-17.05, Piacenza 18.53-19.30, Arquata 1.07-3.05, Sampierdarena 3.44-8.00, Savona 9.50-10.49, Ventimiglia 16.30-18.58	
	6		Cannes 21.54-0.14, Marseille 8.09-8.15, Nevers 9.57-12.44.	
	8		Avignon 16.18-16.53, Les Laps 20.41-21.49, Lyon Vaise 4.32-5.50	
			Chalon 9.56-10.21, Beaune 11.25-12.05, Dijon 13.19-13.50, Le Laumes 16.38-17.25	
			St. Florentin 20.13-8.90, Longueau 2.3.13, Mondicourt 7½s 8.30	
			On detraining at the last named station the 2nd Bn. Batt.	
			marched to billets at Enclemont when 1st & K.R. Rifles were	
			already stationed, the Remainder of the day was spent in	
			cleaning equipment, arms etc.	3 O.R. Evacuated Sick
	9	9.30am	Company parade for inspection and arm drill	
		11.45am	6.o parade for inspection in fighting order and battalion	
			drill	1 O.R. Evacuated Sick
		2.30pm	Company parade for P.T.	

WAR DIARY
or
INTELLIGENCE SUMMARY

Army Form C. 2118. 23rd Middlesex Regt.

(Erase heading not required.)

Place	Date	Hour	Summary of Events and Information	Remarks and references to Appendices
Boullemont	1918 March 10	10 am	Voluntary Church Service. HUMBERCOURT. Day of Rest.	
"	11	9 am	Two Coys. on Range at LUCHEUX 9am to 5pm. Remainder Batt- Baths.	
			at LUCHEUX and Recreational Training. 3 O.R. Reinforcements. 3 O.R. Evacuated sick.	
"	12	9 am	Brigade Exercise – Open Warfare. Remainder on training Ground at LUCHEUX	
"	13	9 am	Two Coys on Range at LUCHEUX 9am to 5pm. Remainder training on	
			training Ground. Continuation of the 2nd Movement in the Attack	
			Recreational Training. 8 O.R. Reinforcements. 6 O.R. Evacuated sick.	
"	14	8:30am	Batt- allotted Baths at LUCHEUX until 6pm. 2 O.R. Evacuated sick.	
"	15	8 am	Parade allotted to "D" Coy all day. Remainder training. 2 O.R. Evacuated sick.	
		9 am	Two Coys on training Ground. (Subject Duties in Ropes Open Warfare	
		12 noon	Commanding Officers Parade. Batt- Drill.	
"	16	9 am	Brigade Practice Attack with HUMBERCOURT as objective owing to	
			rain operation was not completed. 2 O.R. Reinforcements. 2 O.R. Evacuated sick.	
"	17	9:15 am	Batt- Church Parade. 3 O.R. Reinforcements. 2 O.R. Evacuated sick.	
"	18	9 am	Two Coys on Range until 6 pm. 2 O.R. Evacuated Sick.	
		9 am	Two Coys on Training Ground. "Open Warfare Scheme"	

WAR DIARY

23rd Middlesex Regt

Army Form C. 2118.

or

INTELLIGENCE SUMMARY.

(Erase heading not required.)

Instructions regarding War Diaries and Intelligence Summaries are contained in F.S. Regs., Part II. and the Staff Manual respectively. Title pages will be prepared in manuscript.

Place	Date	Hour	Summary of Events and Information	Remarks and references to Appendices
	1918 MARCH			
COULLEMONT	18	10:14 pm	Brigade Night Concentration March to WARLUZEL. Batt: returned to billets at 11:30 pm.	
"	19	9:30 am	Batt: marched to Training Area at SONCAMP. Training under company arrangements. Afternoon devoted to Recreational Training.	
	20	6:30 am	Range and Baths at LUCHEUX allotted to Batt: all day.	
	21	5:20 am	Batt: marched to MONDICOURT – PAS entraining there at 7 am. Detrained at ALBERT at 3:45 pm. Marched to billets at BOUZINCOURT. 4 O.R. evacuated sick.	
BOUZINCOURT	22	9 am	Batt: marched to ACHIET LE PETIT via MIRAUMONT.	
"		2 pm	Dumps seen on roadside. Blankets dumped. Bowman's ammunition issued to Coys.	
		3:30 pm	Ponies took Batt: (less details) to MONUMENT on ARRAS – BAPAUME ROAD. Bivouaced in field until midnight.	
BEUGNY		12:15 am	Marched to BEUGNY via FREMICOURT to take up support position in front of BEUGNY. Batt: disposed in shelters or Railway trenches by dawn. B.H.Q. – cellar in BEUGNY.	

WAR DIARY or INTELLIGENCE SUMMARY.

Army Form C. 2118.

23rd Middlesex Regt.

Place	Date	Hour	Summary of Events and Information	Remarks and references to Appendices
BEUGNY	1916 March 22	—	Casualties - 12. O.R. Wounded, 2 Killed - 2 Missing by Bomb at 2nd Bn S.R. Midlands Wounded at Rail camp	
"			S. O.R. Rejoined Bn.	
"	23rd	10.30 pm	Enemy heavily bombarded BEUGNY. Also shelled our positions to the left of village. Enemy attacked Battalion retired to avoid to live on right and left flanks. "D" Coy. covered the retirement by rapid fire and rifle New line (GREEN LINE) taken up astride BEUGNY-FREMICOURT ROAD. Relieved on night 23/24 and bivouaced near outskirts of FAVREUIL.	
"			Casualties on 23rd - 3 Killed, 36 Wounded, 12 Missing, 1 missing felt Killed. 3 missing felt wounded. 1 evacuated sick.	
FAVREUIL	24th	11.30 am	Took up Reserve line near FAVREUIL to the rear of HIN DUMP site in the afternoon by front line commenced a retirement reaching the Reserve line where they were re-organised and placed into position in the Battalion. At 9 pm orders were received to withdraw to a new line at MONUMENT. This was done - His men digging in conjunction with R.E. while claim. Casualties on 24th - 13 Killed, 54 Wounded, 6 Missing. 6 Missing to Missing 2 Killed. 22 Missing 2 Wounded.	

Army Form C. 2118.

WAR DIARY
or
INTELLIGENCE SUMMARY. 23rd Battⁿ Middlesex Regt.

(Erase heading not required.)

Place	Date	Hour	Summary of Events and Information	Remarks and references to Appendices
MONUMENT	MARCH 1918 25.	5 AM	Shelling of our line commenced. Enemy attacked shortly afterwards compelling the troops to withdraw across the ARRAS - BAPAUME ROAD to the line held by the Battⁿ. The enemy continued to push forward in great formation & was not until the units on both left & right had taken that the Battⁿ commenced an orderly withdrawal by platoons. Casualties were heavy and the enemy pushed the trenches in considerable numbers as Battⁿ H.Q. commenced to withdraw. During the day 6 For Wins were taken and D Coys Battalion entrainment behind BIHUCOURT.	
			(b) ACHIET - LE - PETIT. The survivors who retired during the night 25/26. The Battalion assembled (via BUCQUOY) at GOMME COURT and took up a reserve line in the trenches there for the night. Casualties on the 25th: 13 Killed, 61 Wounded, 30 Missing Wounded & Killed, Missing believed wounded.	
			Killed. 2ⁿᵈ Lt W.D. Tull. 2ⁿᵈ Lt T.J. Pitty.	
			Wounded. a/Capt W. Hammond M.C. Lieut-R.A. Green 2ⁿᵈ Lt L. Barton.	
			Missing Believed Killed. Lt-Col A.R. Haig-Brown D.S.O. Missing 1/Acpt BT Yoss M.C.	
			Evacuated Sick. 2ⁿᵈ Lt J. Jennings.	

A6945 Wt. W14422/M1160 350,000 12/16 D. D. & L. Forms/C./2118/14.

WAR DIARY
or
INTELLIGENCE SUMMARY.

23rd Battn Middlesex Regt. Army Form C. 2118.

(Erase heading not required.)

Place	Date	Hour	Summary of Events and Information	Remarks and references to Appendices
BEINVILLIERS	MARCH 1918 26		Battn moved to BEINVILLIERS and bivouaced for the night. Men had	
"	"		a hot meal. 1 O.R. missing.	
"	27		Battn moved to a line at GOMME COURT and the same night moved	
			yet again and went into trenches at ESSARTS. 5 O.R. evac. sick	
ABLAINZAVILLE	28		Battn moved forward and took up position in support. Battalion	
			at ABLAINZAVILLE. 2 O.R. wounded	
"	29		Remained support Battn " 4 OR Wounded	
"	30		" " "	
"	31		Went into front line at ABLAINZAVILLE. 5 O.R. Wounded. 1 missing	
			Relieved wounded.	

Bertram Hewett
Lt Col
Comdg. 23rd Middlesex Regt.

41st Division.
123rd Infantry Brigade

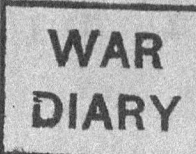

23rd BATTALION

THE MIDDLESEX REGIMENT

APRIL 1918

WAR DIARY
INTELLIGENCE SUMMARY. 23 Batt Middlesex Regt.

Army Form C. 2118.

Vol 24

Place	Date	Hour	Summary of Events and Information	Remarks and references to Appendices
ABLAINZEVILLE	APRIL 1st 1918	—	Batt occupied front line. Considerable shelling on the part of the enemy. French Mortars effective and shot on Vieven Huts occupied by the enemy about 500 yards Nth front. 1.O.R. wounded.	
"	2nd		Front line, Uneventful day. Relieved by 10th Manchesters and proceeded to BIENVILLIERS. Men were served with hot-meal. 1.O.R. evacuated sick	
BIENVILLIERS	3rd		Batt taken by motor lorries to THIEVRES early in the morning. Balance of Batt de-bussed & went on a second journey. Was made to BONNIERE where men were billeted.	
BONNIERE	4th	1.20AM	Marched to FREVENT STATION. [strikethrough] A short march to FREVENT.	
		3.30AM	Entrained and detrained at HOPOUTRE — POPERINGHE. Was convey by Batt to EECKE where all companies were billeted. Bn HQrs at St SYLVESTER CAPEL. 30/p. 316 O.R. reinforcements	
EECKE	5th		Inspection by Army Commander. Baths at CAESTRE	
"	10—		Baths and cleaning up. 3. O.R. Reinforcements. 8 O.R. evacuated sick	
"	"		Training and Parades. 1 O.R. Reinforcements. 5 O.R. evacuated sick	
EECKE	6		Marched to STEENVORDE Station and entrained. Detrained at ST JEAN	

WAR DIARY
INTELLIGENCE SUMMARY. 23rd Batt= Middlesex Regt.

Army Form C. 2118.

Place	Date	Hour	Summary of Events and Information	Remarks and references to Appendices
	1916 April			
JUNCTION CAMP	8th		Marched to JUNCTION CAMP and IRISH CAMP. Billeted in huts.	
	9th		Batt= moved to front-line. 1 Coy- posts in front-line. 1 Coy at INCH HOUSES - 1 Coy at KRONPRINZ and 1 Coy at ENGLISH FARM. BATT= HQs in PILLBOX 83. Batt= relieved 5th Worcesters of 29th Divn. Relief difficult on account of darkness.	
FRONT LINE	10th		Fairly heavy shelling. 1.O.R. Wounded	
"	11th		1.O.R. evacuated	
"	12th		1.O.R evacuated. On the night 12/13th the Batt= was relieved by 10th R.W.Kents. The front line became an outpost line and the Batt= withdrew to PLUM and RAT KEEPS - in the main Line of resistance.	
PLUM KEEP	13th		Men dug all day improving positions. 7.O.R. evacuated.	
"	14th		Digging continued. On the night of 14/15th the Batt= sent one company to relieve WIELTJE - POTIZJE Line. One company remained in PLUM KEEP as outposts. 1.O.R evacuated.	
WIELTJE	15th		Batt= at work on new line - 6.O.R. reinforcements. 12.O.R. Evacuated	
"	16th		Digging continued	

WAR DIARY
or
INTELLIGENCE SUMMARY. 23rd Batt. Middlesex Regt.

Army Form C. 2118.

Place	Date	Hour	Summary of Events and Information	Remarks and references to Appendices
WEILTJE	April 14th		Digging continued. Company in front line carried out patrol to HILL 35	
"	15th		2ND LT. J.M. Morrison wounded. 1 O.R. wounded. Same dispositions	
"	16th		" " Company on outpost - handed over road on HILL 35 which was taken and held again during the same day	
"			2ND LT R.E. MOORHOUSE killed. 2 O.R. Killed. 1 O.R. Wounded. 7. O.R. Missing. 3. O.R. Reinforcements.	
"	20th		3. O.R. Evacuated	
"	21st		1 O.R. Reinforcement. 2. O.R. Evacuated	
"	22nd		5 O.R. Evacuated	
"	23rd		LT. COL. B.A. SMITH M.C. Joined Batt. Capt. J.A. LAIDLAW evac. sick 2nd Lt. A.G. Stewart. - 2nd Lt. T.J. Gregory. 2nd Lt. B.K. Kay joined.	
"	24th		1 O.R. missing 4. O.R. evacuated	
"	25th		Outpost company brought down enemy aeroplane. 2 airmen captured with 2 M.G's. 2nd Lt. R. Cunningham & 2nd Lt. G.B. Gifford joined Batt. 1 O.R. Reinforcements. 5 O.R. Evacuated sick. 1 O.R. Wounded.	

Army Form C.2118.

WAR DIARY
or
INTELLIGENCE SUMMARY. 23rd Batt. Middlesex Regt.
(Erase heading not required.)

Place	Date	Hour	Summary of Events and Information	Remarks and references to Appendices
WIELTJE	1917 APRIL 26	5a	Outpost line withdrawn. Main line of resistance became new outpost line. Batt. withdraws to new positions at V3 near MACHINE GUN FARM. Lt Col Meakin 2ic - A/g Barclay - A/A Wilmot - WHS Doolo anet V.G. Vice Jones Butler Wall 90.6.9 Paid evacuated sick. 4 O.R. wounded	
"	27	6a	4 O.R. evacuated sick – 1 O.R. Reinforcement	
V.3			War line unwired. Explosion of dump near Que Store & camp. 1 O.R. killed, 2 Wounded. 12 O.R. evacuated sick.	
"	28		Work Parties	
"	29		Work Parties	
"	30		Three Huts shelled. 2 O.R. killed + 10 R. wounded. 24 - O.R. Peckart Evacuated sick. Strength: O/ts: 28, O.R. 620	

Lieut Col
Commander 23rd Middlesex Regt

WAR DIARY or INTELLIGENCE SUMMARY

Army Form C. 2118.

23rd Middlesex Regt

Place	Date	Hour	Summary of Events and Information	Remarks and references to Appendices
Reserve area V4	1/5/18		Battalion in brigade reserve, working on the defences of V4. One Company	1 OR Reinforcement
I.6.d			1/2 Platoon, 2 Companies attached to 10 R.W. Kents for duty in front line.	
"	2/5/18		Remaining 2 companies on nights, working on defences of V4. Battalion area	
"	3/5/18		heavily shelled.	Capt H.S. John S.B. wounded Lieut. 4 OR wounded
" Nieske	3/5/18-4/5/18		Battalion relieved outpost line from 10 R.W. Kents	18 Cow Evac 4 OR wounded
Outpost line	4/5/18 to		Battalion holding outpost line C.28.c – C.28.a – I.4.6 Defences strengthened	4th 5 OR Reinforcements
				5th 4 OR Reinforcements
	10/5/18		On 8th 10/5/18 an E.A. brought down by our L.G. fire	6th 5 OR Evac. sick
Night 10/5/18 – 11/5/18			Battalion relieved by 2nd R. Innisks Fus. Moved back to	7th 5 OR 2 OR Evac sick
Warrington Camp H.2.c			Warrington Camp H.2.c	8th 3 OR Wounded
Warrington Camp 11/5/18			Rest and baths	9th 5 OR Evac sick
Orrilla Camp H.2.w	12/5/18		Battalion and working party Church Parade. Moved to Orrilla Camp H.2.a	10th 3 OR Evac sick
"	13/5/18		Digging the defences on the yellow line. 14 OR Reinforcements	11th 3 OR 67 NCOs to English Base
"	14/5/18		ditto 6 OR Reinforcements	(Major L.F. Poland M.C. returned from command)
"	15/5/18		ditto 15 OR Evac sick	
"	16/5/18		Training and baths with the exception of one company on carrying. 30 OR Reinforcements	13 OR Reinforcements
	17/5/18		Inspection of Gas arrangements by Commanding Officer	10 ? Evac. sick
				2/Lt D.W. Pickett to English Base

WAR DIARY
INTELLIGENCE SUMMARY
(Erase heading not required.)

Army Form C. 2118.

23RD MIDDLESEX REGT

Place	Date	Hour	Summary of Events and Information	Remarks and references to Appendices
	Night 17/18 May		Battalion went into the line in brigade reserve in YPRES DEFENCES	
YPRES DEFENCES	18/19/20 to 21/5/18		R.J. 28 N.W. I.20.d.5.3. to I.18.d.5.1. Relieving 12 O.E. Surrey Regt. Battalion in brigade reserve. Work carried out on own defences. Work parties also supplied each night to work on forward lines	18th 5 OR Evac. Sick. 2 OR wounded 1 Reinforcement 19th 89 OR Reinforcements 20th 1 OR wounded
	Night 21/22 May		Battalion taken over the Right sector 1 Brigade front line from the 11th Batt. Queens. I.4.d.00.20. to I.10.c.50.60.	5 OR Evac sick 4/13 B.C. Stokes – joined Regt H.C. DRAWN 2/Lt C.R.T. FLINT (RF) " A.W. STOKES " F.V. WILLIS " A.A. WILMOTT ENGLAND – 2 OR Reinforcements Batt
Front line	22/5/18		Bn. in same line. Reconnoitring patrols to WEST Fm. THATCH Fm. BOUNDARY Fm.	3 OR Reinforcement
"	23/5/18		ditto	
"	24/5/18		ditto – Railway cutting. No 1 Rifle Fm	1 OR wounded died of wounds
"	25/5/18		ditto – WEST Fm. THATCH Fm. BOUNDARY Fm.	2 OR Reinforcements 3 OR Reinforcements 2 OR died of wounds
"	26/5/18		ditto Fighting patrols to Railway cutting No 1 Rifle Fm	5 OR Reinforcements 1 OR wounded 2 OR Evac sick
"	27/5/18		ditto DILLY FARM	
"	28/5/18		ditto "	
	Night 29/30 May		Bn. relieved by 10th R.W.Kent G. March back to YPRES DEFENCES	7 OR Evac Sick 2 OR wounded
YPRES DEFENCES	30/5/18		Bn. in brigade reserve. Work carried out on defences and parties on same	14 OR Reinforcement 1 OR wounded
	31/5/18		"	2 OR Reinforcements 1 OR wounded

Trench Strength 24 Officers 636 Other Ranks

Comdg 23rd Middlesex Regt

23 Middlesex
Stone
Vol 26

WAR DIARY or INTELLIGENCE SUMMARY
Army Form C. 2118.

(Erase heading not required.)

Place	Date	Hour	Summary of Events and Information	Remarks and references to Appendices
YPRES	June 1st		Battalion in Brigade Reserve at YPRES DEFENCES. Work carried on on our defences, & parties supplied for to return on forward lines.	
"	2nd		cwMo	
"	2/3		Battalion relieved by 2/4th K.O.Y.L.I's. Battalion proceeded back to SCHOOL CAMP at ST JAN TER BIESEN.	
ST JAN TER BIESEN	4th		Battalion entrained at PROVEN & detrained at WATTEN & marched to ST MOMELIN area for training & current rest.	
ST MOMELIN	5th		Battalion resting & generally cleaning up.	
"	6th		Training under Company arrangements & baths.	
"	7th		cwMo	
"	8th			
"	9th		Battalion parade, Brigadier present, he addressed the men. Church parade in evening, Brigadier present, and the unit	
"	10th		Battalion moved by motor lorries to ST MARTIN-AU-LAERT.	
ST MARTIN-AU-LAERT	11th		Training under company arrangements.	
"	12th		cwMo Lecture by Divisional Commander to all Officers.	

Stone

WAR DIARY
INTELLIGENCE SUMMARY
(Erase heading not required.)

Army Form C. 2118.

Place	Date	Hour	Summary of Events and Information	Remarks and references to Appendices
ST. MARTIN AU LAERT.	June 13th		Training under Company arrangements & Ca.H.Q.	
"	14th		Training under Company arrangements on Battalion Musketry area.	
"	15th		"Bullet & Bayonet" competition on "A" Range. A platoon of "B" Company won the Battalion competition.	
"	16th		Church Parade taken by Asst Chaplin General. The Brigade competition of the "Bullet & Bayonet" competition held on "A" Range.	
"	17th		Battalion distance judging & aiming on training area.	
"	18th		Brigade scheme on training area.	
"	19th		Company training on training area.	
"	20th		Battalion firing on "A" Range.	
"	21st		Training under company arrangements & Baths.	
"	22nd		Ferry Field Practice on "A" Range.	
"	23rd		Church Parade taken by Assistant Chaplin General.	
"	24th		Battalion training on training area.	
"	25th		Battalion moved by route march to NIEURLET near ST MOMELIN.	
NIEURLET	26th		Battalion moved by route march to ZERMEZEELE near ARNEKE.	

WAR DIARY Store

~~INTELLIGENCE SUMMARY.~~

Army Form C. 2118.

Place	Date	Hour	Summary of Events and Information	Remarks and references to Appendices
ZERMEZEELE	27		Training under company arrangements.	
"	28		Training under company arrangements. Baths.	
"	29		Baths & Battalion Sports.	
"	30		Batt" moved from Zermezeele (by route march) to Wippenhoek.	

WAR DIARY

INTELLIGENCE SUMMARY

23rd Batt. Middlesex Regt.

Vol 27

Army Form C. 2118.

Place	Date	Hour	Summary of Events and Information	Remarks and references to Appendices
	1918			
WIPPENHOEK	July 1/2		Battⁿ proceeded to Kemmel front and relieved French troops in front System.	
KEMMEL	" 2/3		Battⁿ H.Q. at N.7.C.13.24.	
KEMMEL	" 3/4		Battⁿ carried on work in defences in front line.	
"	" 4/5		Battⁿ Headquarters moved to M.12.C.92.23. Work carried out on defences.	
"	" 5/6		Battⁿ carried on work on own defences in front line and Firwerry Tap.	
"	" 6/7		Battⁿ relieved by 11th Battⁿ Bn/eusen and took over the Brigade Reserve Line from 10th Battⁿ R.W. Kents.	
Kasteel M.17.				
Kasteel M.17.	" 7/8		Work carried out on the Westoutre - Goet Moets M.17 Line	
"	" 8/9		" " " " " " and Bathing	
"	" 9/10		" " " " " " , cable burying and Bathing	
"	" 10/11		" " " " " " and cable burying	
La Clytte	" 11/12		Battⁿ proceeded to Support Line of front System and relieved 10th Battⁿ R.W. Kents. Wiring and trench digging under R.E. supervision.	

Army Form C. 2118.

WAR DIARY
INTELLIGENCE SUMMARY.
(Erase heading not required.)

Instructions regarding War Diaries and Intelligence Summaries are contained in F. S. Regs., Part II. and the Staff Manual respectively. Title pages will be prepared in manuscript.

Place	Date	Hour	Summary of Events and Information	Remarks and references to Appendices
La CLYTTE	12/13 July		Left Rt C.T. check-boarded to Batt. H.Q. Wiring and trench clearing under R.E. supervision.	
"	13/14 "		Fire-Steps fitted to trenches of left front Coy. Wiring and trench-digging under R.E. supervision. Heavy shelling from 7.45 a.m. to 8.45 a.m. blew in parts of the trenches.	
"	14/15 "		Work as 13/14 "	
"	15/16 "		" " 14/15 " Two Patrols went out with R.W. Kents.	
KEMMEL	16/17		Relieved 10th Batt. Royal West Kents in front line. Two patrols operated in NO-mans-Land. (See reports) American details joined for instruction.	
"	17/18		Work carried out on enemy defences and wiring under R.E. supervision. Two Patrols as above. American for instruction.	
"	18/19		Work and Patrols as on 17/18.	
"	19/20		Work and Patrols as on 18/19. 11th Queens raided enemy posts on our front.	
"	20/21		" " " " 19/20. American details were replaced.	
"	21/22		" " " " 20/21. Enemy captured one of our advanced posts.	

G.D. Smith, M.C. proceeded on leave.

WAR DIARY
or
INTELLIGENCE SUMMARY.
(Erase heading not required.)

Army Form C. 2118.

Instructions regarding War Diaries and Intelligence Summaries are contained in F. S. Regs., Part II. and the Staff Manual respectively. Title pages will be prepared in manuscript.

Place	Date	Hour	Summary of Events and Information	Remarks and references to Appendices
Wippenhoek Area:-	July 22/23		Relieved by 11th Queens and took over the 124 Bde Reserve Billets from the 26th Royal Fusiliers. B.H.Q. at E.30.a.90.05.	
"	23/24		Cleaning up and work on the Westoutre line under R.E supervision	
"	24/25		Baths at E.32.d.22. and E.29.c.8.2. Working party under R.E supervision	
"	25th		Working parties under R.E Supervision. Kit inspection, recommencing	
"	26th		" " " " " Cleaning up.	
"	27th		The Brigadier inspected companies.	
"	28th		Divine Service at "A" Coy Billets	
"	29th		Working party of 100 men under R.E supervision on the WESTOUTRE LINE	
"	29th		Delousing at Divisional Bathing Station at K.29.3.7.7.	
"	30th		Three companies cable-burying under div signalling officer. One company on the Westoutre Line under R.E Supervisor.	
"	31st		Two companies working on the Westoutre Line and 2 companies being inspected	

WAR DIARY or INTELLIGENCE SUMMARY

Army Form C.2118

23 Middlesex Vol 28

Place	Date	Hour	Summary of Events and Information	Remarks and references to Appendices
SHEET 24 L30 a.90 a.05	1918 Aug. 1		Battn. moved to Dallington Camp L.29.c.8.2. Cable Burying by A Coy 10pm – 3am 2 & 3 Aug	
DALLINGTON	2		2nd Battn. 105th American I.R. joined us forming two Composite Battn Groups	
CAMP			equally distributed between "MODO A" and "MODO B"	
MERTMEL	2/3		"A" Battn. Modo relieved 10th Battn. R.W.Kent Regt. in Support Line and B Battn	
"			Modo relieved 3rd Battn. 106th American I.R. in front line	
"	3/4		Work carried out on our defences under R.E. supervision	
"	4/5		"	
"	5/6		Inter-Company Relief	
"	6/7		American troops in front line, Middx in Support. Colonel B.A.Smith M.C.	
"			returned from leave	
"	7/8		Bucklaiding. Resting, training, Lunch bogging and Brig Out construction	
"			under R.E. supervision	
"	8/9		"	
"	9/10		"	
"	10/11		Relieved from Support line by 11th Battn. Queens Regt. Battn. proceed to	
LOYE			Reserve Billets at LOYE and Remy H.Q. at R.3.a.7.6. Cleaning up.	

WAR DIARY

INTELLIGENCE SUMMARY

(Erase heading not required.)

Army Form C. 2118.

Instructions regarding War Diaries and Intelligence Summaries are contained in F.S. Regs., Part II. and the Staff Manual respectively. Title pages will be prepared in manuscript.

Place	Date	Hour	Summary of Events and Information	Remarks and references to Appendices
LOYE	1918 Aug. 12		Baths and Training as per Programme	
"	13		Working Parties – HEKSKEN	
"	14		" " "	
"	15		Corps General's visit. Training proceeded with	
"	16		Brigadier General's visit " "	
"	17		Training Programme followed	
"	18		Voluntary Church Parades	
KEMMEL	18/19		Battn relieved 109th Amer. I.R. in front line	
"	19/20		M.G. Post located by Patrol	
"	20/21		Trench improvements and New Work carried out under R.E. supervision	
"	21/22		on our defences	
"	22/23		" "	
"	23/24		Work ditto. Inter-Company Relief. S.O.S. signal on left sector	
"	24/25		" Listening Post located by Patrol	
"	25/26		Work carried out on our defences	
NORTH OF LA CLYTTE	26/27		Relieved by 26th Battn R.Fusiliers. New Suffolk line taken over from	

A6945 Wt. W14422/M1160 350,000 12/16 D.D.&L. Forms/C./2118/14

WAR DIARY
or
INTELLIGENCE SUMMARY
(Erase heading not required.)

Army Form C. 2118.

Place	Date	Hour	Summary of Events and Information	Remarks and references to Appendices
N of LA CLYTTE	1918 Aug 26/27		Hants Regt. H.Q. at M.G.d.4.6. Baths at Dallington Camp "A" Coy.	
"	28		Baths at Dallington Camp "B" Coy. Work carried out on own defences under R.E. supervision.	
"	28/29		Left Batt. attached to 10th R.W.Kent Regt. in front line for one day.	
"	29/30		Battn. relieved by 4th Batts. Royal Sussex Regt. and entrained at Abeele Station for St Omer. Marched to St Martin au Laert and	
St MARTIN	31		took over billets. Baths. Capt. Bent returned. Cleaning up and clothing inspection, baths.	

Lieut Col R.A.
23 Middlesex Regt

123/41 23 Middx
Army Form C. 2118.

WO 29

WAR DIARY
or
INTELLIGENCE SUMMARY.
(Erase heading not required.)

Instructions regarding War Diaries and Intelligence Summaries are contained in F. S. Regs., Part II. and the Staff Manual respectively. Title pages will be prepared in manuscript.

Place	Date	Hour	Summary of Events and Information	Remarks and references to Appendices
St Martin AU (Linest.)	1918 Sept. 1		Church Parade at Trenfontaines. Voluntary Services at School - (RAP)	
"	2		Marched to H.Omer. Italian Entrained for Alembe. Italian Passes carried. Stated for tea then proceeded (by Route March) to "Overdom" G.36.g.1. Troops Leaders proceeded on leave	
"	3		Batt. working on own defences	
OUDERDOM	4		Training and reconnoitering Goe Mod. Mu Line	
"	5/6		Relieved East Surrey's and K.R.R's in Brigade Front	
"	6		Batt. working on own defences	
"	7		" "	
"	8		" "	
"	9/10		Relieved by 11th Queen's Regt. and Batt. moved into Support Line. Thereafter proceeded to Transport lines for rest.	
"	10		Batt. working on own defences and accommodation	
"	11		"D" Coy rested for rest	
"	12/13		Batt. working on own defences and accommodation. Baths	
"	13		Batt. relieved the 10th R.W.Kents on left Brigade front.	
"	14/15		" " working on own defences	
"			Relieved by East Lancs. + Batt. move back in reserve to Micro Farm + Ouderdom.	

A6945 Wt. W14421/M160 350,000 12/16 D. D. & L. Forms/C./2118/14.

Army Form C. 2118.

WAR DIARY
or
INTELLIGENCE SUMMARY.
(Erase heading not required.)

Instructions regarding War Diaries and Intelligence Summaries are contained in F. S. Regs., Part II. and the Staff Manual respectively. Title pages will be prepared in manuscript.

Place	Date	Hour	Summary of Events and Information	Remarks and references to Appendices
OUDERDOM	Sept. 16		Battn on working party reconstructing Fife Ave G36. Baths at Busseboom.	
"	17		" " " " " " " " " Burgomy Castle near Hallebast Corner.	
"	18		Working Party (G.9.D.1.1)	
WIPPENHOEK	19		Battn moves to Wippenhoek Lieut. Lewis returned from leave.	
"	20		Fifty men told Working Party. Remainder of Battn training. Company arrangements (Reserves to Poperinghe 5/8)	
"	21		Fifty men on working party. Remainder of Battn training. Battn concert at Y.M.C.A. Remy.	
"	22		Church Parade at Transport Lines. Baths at Ballington Camp.	
"	23		Battn training under Coy. arrangements. Baths. Battn Concert at Y.M.C.A. Remy.	
"	24		" " " " " " " concentration	
"	25		Battalion commenced Brigade Scheme but owing to weather cancelled until 26th Batt.	
"			Football match between "A" & "B" Coys. Result "A" 3 "B" 3. Battn concert at Y.M.C.A. Remy.	
"	26		Brigade Scheme	
"	27		Battn moves to Dominion Camp	
"	28		Reserves from Dominion Camp to Ambulance Farm with Brewery Reserve to Devon.	
			Moves from Ambulance Farm to Battle Wood	
	29		Moves from Battle Wood to Devonport Tunnel. All Carried out according to report prepared by Col. Smith.	

A645 Wt. W11442/M160. 350,000 12/16 D.D.&L. forms/C/2118/14

WAR DIARY
or
INTELLIGENCE SUMMARY.

Army Form 8.

Place	Date	Hour	Summary of Events and Information	Remarks and references to Appendices
	Sept 30.	12.n.	472nd Borgues Farm Keiegh and Tyrsdeeri subsequently the batts. withdrew to dulluk. P.27.c.	(in reserve). Sheet 28. Right... Histon Funk D.6.L. Centre 23 - Division

From :- O.C. 23rd Middlesex Regiment.

To :- Headquarters,
123rd Inf. Brigade.

REPORT ON OPERATION CARRIED OUT ON 29/9/18.

I beg to report as follows on the above operation :-

The orders which I recived from you at 12.30.a.m. instructed me to advance on a frontage of 700 yards my Right on the CANAL as shown in green on plan. Commencing at 5.30.a.m., with 10th R.W. KENTS on my Left I was to advance 4000 yards and pass through the 124th Inf. Brigade and gain the first and second objective as shown on map in yellow and red.

After passing through 124th Inf. Brigade I was to protect my Right Flank by putting out Posts along the CANAL, and I was to get in touch with the XVth Corps in square V3.

I understood that I was responsible for the protection of my Right until I gained touch with the XVth Corps and that my Left was protected by the 10th R.W. KENTS, and their Left by other troops. I had attached to me 1 Trench Mortar with 30 rounds ammunition and 1 section of Machine Guns.

The Battalion marched from my Bivouac in I.36.c. at 4.0.a.m. and moved in single file as marked on map. The ground was very broken, full of shell holes and at one place a great deal of traffic was encountered and it was exceedingly difficult to keep direction. The Battalion however arrived at 6.6.c.9.6. on the Right of the R.W. KENTS who were already drawn up at 5.10.a.m. and I at once deployed, and the advance commenced at 5.30.a.m. The formation I adopted in this advance wereCoys. in "diamond formation". My Leading Company, Lt. C.T. MEESTER, Advance Guard, with his Company, with 2 platoons in depth moving in section artillery formation. One company marched on the right near the Railway and one on the Left, both in Platoon Artillery formation, and my fourth Company in Support moving behind also in the same formation.

The Trench Mortar I attached to my leading Company, and I intended to keep the M.G. Section in hand, but they did not turn up until very much later in the day. My H.Q. moved roughly in the centre of the Battalion.

The instructions which I gave to my leading Company were to push through to the first objective, and if after passing through the 124th Inf. Brigade I considered his front too large for him to manage, I would push up my Left Flank Company to assist him. My Right Flank Coy. had instructions to put out posts along the CANAL BANK as soon as the 124 Brigade had been passed. The fourth Company I intended to keep in hand.

The advance which commenced in the dark was carried out in good order, direction and touch were well maintained.

On two occasions there was slight difficulty owing to one Company of 10th R.W. KENTS squeezing in on to my front.

This Coy. as soon as it got Light I found on the Railway, on my Right, and I passed it through my Battalion to rejoin its own unit, this manoeuvre did not cause any confusion to my advance.

On arriving at N.W. side of KORTEWILDE we came across the 124th Brigade, and then found that that had been their extreme advance the night before, and that they had not reached the Line which I was led to expect.

They were however just commencing to move forward.

KORTEWILDE was held lightly by Bosche and it was taken as we arrived there.

The 124th Brigade then halted by the R.E. Dump at HOUTHEM, and my Battalion went through the 10th QUEENS and some of the 20th D.L.I. my Trench Mortar clearing HOUTHEM village.

The advance from this Point onwards for 2000 yards was exceedingly rapid, prisoners being freely taken, and opposition slight. There was, however, a considerable amount of M.G. fire from West side of the CANAL, which caused a certain number of casualties. After passing HOUTHEM, one platoon of my Leading Coy. under Sgt. POTTS crossed the CANAL to exploit success, and returned with 35 prisoners and 3 Machine Guns.

Another Platoon of this Company under 2/Lt. E.C. GIFFARD collected some 50 prisoners. As the result of the delay caused to this Company by these manoeuvres, my front became uncovered, and I had also lost touch with the Battalion on my Left, except for one Company which was constantly coming across my front. I therefore pushed forward my Reserve Company to cover my advance, and by 10.0.a.m. my Headquarters were establsihed on the Railway bank at P.27.c.9.5.

My Right Flank Company had established posts all along the Railway, taking up strong positions and were able to make good use of their Rifles and Lewis Guns at frequent targets which the Bosche offered them.

My leading Company lining the Road from the CANAL towards KORENTJE where they captured 3 Field Guns, 2 machine guns and 1 Light Machine Gun. Beyond this point I was unable to proceed and was held up by heavy Machine Gun fire both from the front and from the West of the CANAL.

My Left Flank Company which had lost touch with the R.W. KENTS except for 2 platoons, who were with them, endeavoured to push up and make good the Left Flank, but were held up by Machine Gun fire in P.27.c. My original leading Company had by this time reformed, and I sent them forward to try and outflank Machine Gun and reach the final objective. This they were unable to do and suffered a good many casualties.

At 12 noon it became clear that we were up against considerable opposition and casualties became frequent. I therefore moved back my Headquarters to P.27.a.1.5. where the Machine Gun Officer reported to me.

I told him to bring overhead fire to bear, to try to enable my Left flank Company to advance, but no benefit was derived from this. At this stage parties of Bosche were reported coming out to attack my Left flank which was in the air, and Machine Gun fire increased in intensity.

I therefore withdrew my line to approx. P.27.a.1.5. running along the stream and covering the road to a point about P.27.a.5.8.

At this point there was considerable activity and the men were fighting well and using their weapons to good effect. Machine Gun fire was heavy and I became exceedingly anxious about my Left flank. I had had no communication from the KENTS, but I fortunately ascertained where Col. THESIGER'S Headquarters were and went across to find out his dispositions on my Left.

I found this officer at P.20.d.3.5. where I established my Headquarters so as to be in close touch with him.

I found that his left flank was certainly in the air, and I was not satisfied that his Battalion was really covering my left flank.

Things at 3.0.p.m. began to look exceedingly bad, the Bosche were working rapidly round with Machine Guns on the Left, a threatened attack was reported by my Company Commander on the Railway on my Right, and the DURHAM LIGHT INFANTRY on the Railway further back sent up similar information. A Bosche aeroplane commenced to fly low over the area dropping lights and drawing artillery fire. Ammunition began to give out and casualties were severe. I became very anxious for the Left Flank of my Battalion quite apart from the Battalion on my Left, and at this point, so as to have a reserve in hand, I withdrew Lt. C.T. MEESTER'S Company from firing line which when carried out gave me a reserve in hand with my Headquarters, with which, if things became worse I should be able to form a defensive flank on my left, and gradually withdraw my front Companies. This difficult manoeuvre of withdrawing a Company from the firing line was ably carried out in good order, in spite of heavy casualties, by Lt. C.T. MEESTER. The situation was so unsatisfactory that I again conferred with Col. THESIGER, as the Bosche were working round our flank still more actively, and we decided to bring back the left and form a line just in front of my Batt. Headquarters in P.20.d. and Col. THESIGER undertook to conform on my Left.

Lt. E.H. SHRAGER disengaged himself from the fight and brought his Company back to this point in most excellent order, where they took up a line across a road which I indicated to him, and the manner in which this was performed was greatly to the credit of this officer, as he had to bring his Company down the road through a mixture of wounded men and others and not one man of his Company required to be rallied.

"C" Company under Major J.A. LAIDLAW conformed on his Right, and kept in touch with Capt. D.J. HAMILTON on the Railway.

One section Machine Guns under Lt. J. HERRIOT did not withdraw, but remained out in the most praiseworthy manner causing great execution to the Bosche and greatly assisting my defence.

Every effort had already been made to get artillery fire and more supplies of S.A.A. S.O.S. Rockets were sent up and pigeons were despatched and things began to look so bad that I decided to withdraw my Right, as well, down the Railway.

In reply to this order however Capt. D.J. HAMILTON reported that large bodies of English troops were coming across from the direction of MESSINES and were within 500 yards of him, and saying that he would not withdraw until he received further orders, and strongly recommending that he should maintain our positions for the present.

At this time 4.0.p.m. our Artillery opened, and I had further information from Capt. D.J. HAMILTON that he was in touch with the 30th Division. In a masterly manner he obtained the assistance of the leading 2 Companies of the leading Battalion, and got them to line the Railway and bring cross fire to bear across our front, which with the artillery support saved the situation. The manner in which this officer appreciated the situation is, in my mind, worthy of the highest praise.

From then onwards the situation rapidly improved although the Machine Gun fire was active and I moved up my left flank to the position from which they had last retired. Further operation were imposible owing to shortage of S.A.A. but my immediate wants were provided by 3 boxes of S.A.A. dropped by aeroplane 20 minutes after they had picked up "V" Signal.

I then took up a line of outposts on instructions I received from you.

The conduct of the Company officers and men throughout the advance and subsequent defence and withdrawal, was most praiseworthy, and I propose making several recommendations for award.

The following captures were made :-
        110 prisoners.
        5 Machine Guns.
        1 Light Machine Gun.
        4 Field Guns.

My Casualties were 5 Officers and 136 men, 25 of the latter being killed.

Heavy casualties were inflicted throughout the day on the enemy.

..........Lt-Col.
Commanding 23rd Middlesex Regiment.

WAR DIARY or INTELLIGENCE SUMMARY

Army Form C.2118.

23rd M[iddlesex] Vol 30

Place	Date	Hour	Summary of Events and Information	Remarks and references to Appendices
	9/24			
	1.		Bath moved from Reserve Willets (Scheubrodt Finals S.W. of Tambenha) From this place moved to Anvers Wood, details of attack as to post forwarded by Colonel	
	2.	2.30 pm	Battn in cooperation with M.M.R & K's advanced "strengthen" line	
	3.		Battn in the line	
	3/4		Battn relieved by the 5th A & S Highlanders (30th Div)	
	4.		Moved to Huts in J.35 area	
	5.		In Huts J.35 area	
	6.	"	"	
	7.		Took over from D.L.I (122 Brigade) K.20.c	
	8.		Battn having under Cos "A" and "B" to "C" Coy moved forward in close support "D"	Relieving 6th Coy
	9.	"	"	
	10.		"A" Coy sent in front line with 11th Queens. Remaining Coys in support (K.28.d K.29.c)	
	11.	"	"A" " in front line "	
	12.	"	"A" " " " 1st relieved at night by East Surreys (122 Bde)	
	12/13		Battn moved to Bivouacs off Menin Road (in York Dump) K.31 (after)	Battn
	13.		In Bivouacs K.31 (after)	"

WAR DIARY
or
INTELLIGENCE SUMMARY
(Erase heading not required.)

Army Form C. 2118.

Instructions regarding War Diaries and Intelligence Summaries are contained in F.S. Regs., Part II. and the Staff Manual respectively. Title pages will be prepared in manuscript.

Place	Date	Hour	Summary of Events and Information	Remarks and references to Appendices
	Oct. 14.		Batt. arrived at 7.30 a.m. to assembling position in Reserve to 122 & 124 Brigades	K.30.d
	15		" in billets K.30.d	
	16		Batt. proceeded by route march to take over from the 36th Divn (9th R.I.F.) in trenches via Morlancourt. C & D Coys front line, A support B reserve	
	17.		Batt. in line	
	18		" "	
	19		Relieved by 35th Divn & Batt. moved to billets outskirts of Courton. M.6.a. Sheet 29.	
	20		Batt. stayed in billets M.6.a. Sheet 29.	
	21		" moved from billets Rivecourt to billets in area N.24.b. Sheet 29	
	22.		Draft arrived at night. Batt. moved into position O.16.c.6.5. to O.16.b.7.7. Sheet 29	
	23.		Batt. attacks at 2.a.m. Details as per report forwarded to Central	
	24		" "	
	25		Rain	

WAR DIARY
or
INTELLIGENCE SUMMARY.
(Erase heading not required.)

Army Form C. 2118.

Place	Date	Hour	Summary of Events and Information	Remarks and references to Appendices
	Oct. 26.		Batt. relieved by 122 Bde. marched to Bivouac in Bourlon H.32.d Sheet 29.	
	27.		Baths. Reclothing and general cleaning up.	
	28.		Batn. provided guard atternoon for the Corps Commander at Bourlon. Draft arrives.	
	29.		Batn. training under Coy arrangements. C.O. inspected Transport. Draft arrives.	
	30.		" " Transport inspected by	
	31.		" "	

William Kiosk? Lt Col.
Comdg 23rd Middlesex Bn.

From O. C. 23rd [BITTELUX]
To H. Q. 23rd Brigade.

REPORT on Operation of October 1st, 1918.

I received orders about 4 p.m. to march my Battalion to AMERICA WOOD Q 7 central, where I was to deploy and move to the ZERO line about Q.8.C. in S.E. direction. I was then to attack on a 400 yard frontage with one Company in front, and the QUEENS would cooperate on rather a larger frontage on my left. I was also to be responsible for the protection of the right flank. The 122nd Brigade was to attack on the left of the 123rd Brigade. Zero hour was fixed for 6. 15 p.m. and Artillery support promised. Two objectives were given me, the ~~first~~ second one on the Railway C.25.A. Two sections Machine Guns were allotted to me. I had time to make the plan clear to my Company Commanders, but they only had time to give a very brief outline to the Platoon Commanders before the march had to commence, and the rank and file knew little or nothing of the plan. The Machine Gun Officers reported to me just as the Battalion moved off, and I told them on arriving at AMERICA WOOD I would give them instructions. The march commenced ½ mile S.W. of TENBRIELEN and I moved with Platoons in single file 50 yards distance at the side of the road. This movement was under the direct observation of the enemy from WERVICQ who at once opened a heavy Artillery fire. My march was somewhat inconvenienced by a Battalion of another Division who were moving on the same road in the same direction. The Artillery fire however drove them to shell holes which greatly assisted my movements. The march was done in excellent order and ranks were well closed up. On arriving at AMERICA CORNER the Artillery fire became very heavy, and I at once started to deploy and change direction S.E. I had arranged to move the Battalion down to the Zero line with Companys in Diamond formation, the right Company being responsible for the right flank.

(1)

Unfortunately the leading Company Commander was severely wounded as the deployment commenced, the other two Subalterns were in the rear of the Company, and nobody knew except the Company Commander (for reasons I have already given) the plan of attack. The enemy's fire all the time was heavy, and it looked at one moment as if there was going to be chaos. However the C.S.M. with great promptitude and gallantry ran forward and took the two leading Platoons in hand, one of the Subalterns came quickly up and I sent my Adjutant to explain matters to the Subaltern. The result was that the deployment continued with very little delay. I met each Company as it arrived at the deployment point to show them the direction, and they each moved steadily forward in their proper places. The change of direction was most satisfactorily done. The Machine Guns did not however turn up having been delayed on the road, and I had to go on without being able to explain matters to these Officers. On moving over the rise on the S.E. of America Wood, the Battalion was met with very heavy Machine Gun cross fire from the right flank, an Artillery barrage was also put down and some gas. In spite of heavy casualties the Battalion moved forward in perfect order and steadiness, keeping excellent direction. My Reserve Company I kept back with me close to the ridge, and at this time I became very anxious owing to the non-appearance of the QUEENS on my left, and it became clear that they could not possibly be at the Zero line by 6.15 p.m. I therefore sent a Runner forward to the leading Company to tell them not to move beyond the Zero line until the QUEENS came up to them. It appears however that by this time two out of my three Company Commanders in front had been wounded, and the Battalion on arriving at the Zero line came across some Bosch whom they dealt with. Having gone about 100 yards further, and casualties being heavy, Capt. Hamilton on his own initiative and before my message arrived, stopped the advance and waited for the QUEENS. It was now nearly dark, and when the QUEENS did arrive about twenty minutes afterwards, they were so cut up that it was clear that a

(2)

further advance was impossible. The 122nd Brigade did not function in this attack owing to receiving orders too late. Capt. Hamilton took command of the line with great skill, dug in and organised the defence.

While this was going on I moved up my H.Q. close to the line, ascertained the situation and duly reported it to my Brigade. My Reserve Company, who had also had many casualties, I did not use.

The Machine Gunners endeavoured with great gallantry to come into action during the advance, but it was impossible for them to do anything. They however subsequently greatly assisted in the defence.

I should like to specially mention 2nd Lt. Abbot and his Trench Mortar section, who, inspite of having no Trench Mortar ammunition, formed his men into an independent rifle section and gave every assistance he possibly could, quite regardless of his personal danger.

Throughout this action we practically had no Artillery support. Casualties :- 10 O.R. killed and 5 Officers and 72 O.R. Wounded.

Bertram Smith
Lt. Col.
Comdg. 23rd Middlesex Regmt.

To:- Headquarters,
      123rd Infantry Brigade.

REPORT on Operations of the 23rd Middlesex Regiment on the 22nd., 24th and 25th October, 1918.

———————

On the evening of the 22nd I received instructions to march my Battalion and deploy on the road at O. 15. C. facing S.E. A frontage of 600 yards was given me, and I was to advance on a two Company frontage at 11. 30. p.m. The 10th Royal West Kents were to cooperate in like manner on the left, and I understood that troops on their left would also cooperate in a night attack. My right was to be on the Canal, and I was informed that I should be protected on that flank by another Division. The objective given me was the HOSKE - HEESTERT road 3000 yards off. I was to move forward to a line 500 yards in front of the deploying line, and remain there until 2. 30. a.m. when the attack was to commence. I was also to relieve any troops of the 122nd Brigade whom I found in the area. It was hoped that a night attack without Artillery support would catch the Bosch napping. The march to the point of deployment was commenced at 8 o'clock, and I arrived there without incident by 10. 30. p.m. Two Companies were detailed for the attack, and were to move forward in Artillery formation. Two Companies I kept in hand in Farms close to my Headquarters. At the time I arrived at the deploying point there was a considerable amount of overhead Machine Gun fire. The night was light. At 11.30 the Companies moved forward and arrived shortly afterwards at the halting place, beyond which they were not to move forward until 2. 30. a.m. Here the relief of the Hants and Surreys of the 122nd Brigade took place. The 122nd Brigade had already attacked on two or three occasions at this spot without success. At 2. 30. a.m. the Companies again moved forward in conjunction with the R.W. Kents, and at once came under Machine Gun fire. They managed to move forward, and clear out two houses occupied by the enemy, one Machine Gun being captured. On arriving on a line from the tunnel at O. 22. D. 32 to O. 23. C. 16., the right hand Company could make no further progress owing to a nest of Machine Guns in front. The left hand Company was unable to proceed so far, being held up in O. 23 A. owing to Machine Gun fire from their left. It then appeared that the R.W. Kents had been able to make very little progress, and thus my left flank was exposed. Several attempts were made to improve the position, and at 5. a.m., the Kents having made no progress, the left hand Company withdrew and consolidated a line about 300 yards in front of the 2. 30. line. The Company on the right also came back about 400 yards and did the same on their right, making good the Canal. The following day Patrols were sent out over the Canal to get in touch with other troops without success, although all information went to prove they were there. On the morning of the 24th at 2. 30. a.m. a second night attack was commenced, with a certain amount of Artillery support. The right Company moved forward to the same place as the night previous. The left Company was more Successful and pushed up within 200 yards of HOOGMOLEN MILL. The Kents also cooperated on the left, but did not get quite so far. Unfortunately the Kents lost several of their Company Commanders, and the men went back, leaving my left flank exposed, and eventually my line withdrew to a line about 100 yards in front of the line held the day previous. I firmly believe that if the Battalion on the left had been able to continue the attack, we should have been able to obtain possession of the Ridge. On the morning of the 25th at 9. a.m. a third attack was ordered. This however was in conjunction with the Corps on the right and left, with a heavy Artillery barrage. A halting place for the barrage was given some 4000 yards in front, and a final objective of about 7000 yards. My frontage was about six or seven hundred yards, and the Queens were attacking on the left of the Brigade front, the 4th Cheshire Regt. of the 34th Division cooperating on the right. My boundaries were somewhat altered, the road running to HOSKE inclusive being my right

boundary. I attacked with two Companies in front, a party of
R. W. Kents as Moppers up for these two leading Companies close
behind them, and two Companies in support. I also had one Section
of Machine Guns, and one light Trench Mortar, and one 18 pounder
Gun attached to me. I also had for barrage purposes an additional
Section of Machine Guns. I arranged for the Section of Machine
Guns and the 18 pounder to shoot at certain points at Zero hour.
The Battalion commenced the attack in excellent order with close
cooperation with the flank Battalions. The Bosch had withdrawn
most of his Guns from our immediate front early in the morning,
and the Ridge at HOOGMOLEN MILL was passed without difficulty.
A light enemy barrage was put down, causing a few Casualties,
and also one Machine Gun from the Tunnel fired across my front,
which however was soon dealt with by the Cheshires. On going
over the rise towards KEIBERGMOLEN certain 18 pounders were shooting
very short, and the troops had difficulty in keeping up with the
Barrage; in fact after topping the rise I do not consider that the
men were really protected by the barrage from then onwards.
Touch at this point was lost with the Queens on the left, who had
met with considerable opposition. On proceeding down the hill
at HOSKE, the Battalion came under heavy Machine Gun fire from the
Railway on the right which the 34th Division had missed in their
advance, and from houses in HOSKE, and along the road to HEESTERT.
The men went forward most gallantly. The two right hand Companies
got close to HOSKE and dealt with the trouble. They were greatly
assisted in this work by the Light Trench Mortar which I sent
forward. The left front Company was held up in the same manner,
and I assisted their advance with fire from my Section of Machine
Guns. It took three hours before all these Guns were dealt with.
I had established my Headquarters at O. 29. B. at 10 a.m. and
remained there during this fight. I also obtained telephone
communication with Brigade. All hope of getting to the halting
place in time for a barrage for a further advance was gone, and

(3)

I consider that the anxiety of the Company Commanders to get forward to the Barrage hindered their work in dealing with the resistance which they met, and that they were in too much of a hurry to push forward in the face of the Machine Guns which required to be dealt with more systematically. At about 11 a.m. I found a Mopping up party of the 34th Division whom I sent down the Railway to make good the ground which had been missed by this Division. The situation at this critical period was ably reported to me by Lieut. Tevey, who twice went forward under heavy fire and made most excellent reconnaissences. At 2 p.m. having crossed the Railway by HOSKE the Companies re-formed and continued the advance. They met with little opposition except from one Farm where a wounded Bosch was captured. They were however all the way troubled by a distant Machine Gun from the left flank. On renewing the advance touch was obtained with the Queens on the left, but the Division on the right having met with no opposition were out of sight. On arriving at the originally arranged halting place, the two rear Companies moved through the leading Companies and continued the advance until they came up to the village of WOFFELSTRAAT when considerable opposition was met with. It was now getting dark, and it was decided to consolidate the line and make the flanks good. It was then ascertained that there was a gap of some six or seven hundred yards between the 41st and the 34th Division on the right. Second Lieut. Prothero, his Company Commander being wounded, with great initiative took his Company, and made good this gap, and joined up with the Cheshire Regiment. Touch was also obtained with the Queens at SPICHTESTRAAT. An outpost line was established with one Company in reserve, and I sent forward the Section of Machine Guns to assist in the defence of the place for the night. I had taken up my Headquarters close to the Railway South of HOSKE, and by 8 p.m. I was able to give full

26^h. dispositions of my line to Brigade. The following day considerable sniping took place from WOFFELSTRAAT, and this village was ultimately

(4)

Captured by the 10th Hants, 150 Bosch having held the village. After the Bosch had withdrawn from AUTRYVE they threw Gas Shells into the place, and as the Civilians came out in the open, they turned Machine Guns on them.

During those Operations, I lost 2 Company Commanders and 3 other Officers and 79 O.R., 9 of whom were killed.

Prisoners captured 16.

Great credit is due to Second Lieut. Prothero and Second Lt. Kemp who suddenly had to take command of their Companies during the advance, for the excellent manner in which they discharged their duties after their Company Commanders had been wounded.

Lt. Col.
Commdg. 23rd Middlesex Regt.

Headquarters,
123rd Infantry Brigade.

NARRATIVE of OPERATIONS from November 8th to November 11th 1918.

The enemy having gone back from the Scheldt, I received orders at 23.59 hours November 8th to march to CASTER. CASTER was reached at 03.30. hours and the Battalion went into Billets. Instructions were received next morning for an attack to be carried out in conjunction with the French on the left and the Royal West Kents on the right. A frontage of 1000 yards was allotted to the Battalion. Zero hour was fixed for 13.00 hours, but as these instructions were not received until 12.15 hours, it was impossible to be on the deploying point in time. The Battalion crossed the river near MEERSCHE, and commenced the advance in conjunction with the Kents at 14.00 hours. The objective, some 2,500 yards off, was reached without incident, and touch was gained with the French on the left. At 18.00 hours I received orders to push forward a further 1,000 yards, which I did, and took up Outpost for the night from R.9. Central to R.15. Central. In this advance, two Companies were in front, one Company in support, and one Reserve, and I had a Section of Machine Guns, and one Trench Mortar at my disposal. On the night of the 9th I received orders to make a further advance of 10,000 yards due East in conjunction with the Kents on the right and the French on the left. This advance was made in the same formation, and commenced at 09.00 hours. No opposition was met with until within 300 yards of the objective, when the Battalion came under Machine Gun fire. I took up Outpost for the night, and gained touch on the flanks with the French and the Kents. During the night the Bosch Machine Guns withdrew. On the morning of the 11th the 124th Brigade advanced through our line, but the Armistice being signed, operations ceased at 11.00 hours.

16/11/18.

Lt. Col.
Commdg. 23rd Middlesex Regt.

WO95/2639

Identification Trace for use with Artillery Map

WO 95/2639

WO 95/2639

23 Middlesex Regt.

Army Form C. 2118.

WAR DIARY
INTELLIGENCE SUMMARY
(Erase heading not required.)

Instructions regarding War Diaries and Intelligence Summaries are contained in F. S. Regs., Part II. and the Staff Manual respectively. Title pages will be prepared in manuscript.

Place	Date	Hour	Summary of Events and Information	Remarks and references to Appendices
Everbecq	1918 Nov 1		Battⁿ moves to Lessinghem	
Lessinghem	2		" training under Company arrangements	
"	3		" " " "	
"	4		" moves to Kleinberg	
Kleinberg	5		" training under Company arrangements	
"	6		" " " "	
"	7		" " " "	
"	8		" " " "	Orders to move as to Vichte/Wallers @ 23.59 pals
"	9		See narrative attached (marks A)	
"	10		Armistice signed and observed Cadets 11.00 hours	
"	11		Reorganisation – cleaning up	
Bootshoek	12		Battⁿ moves to Grammont	
"	13		" cleaning up	
Grammont	14		" "	
"	15		" "	
"	16		Battⁿ moves into Combined Arrangements - Baths	

A6945 Wt. W11422/M1160 350,000 12/16 D. D. & L. Forms/C./2118/14

WAR DIARY
INTELLIGENCE SUMMARY.
(Erase heading not required.)

Place	Date	Hour	Summary of Events and Information	Remarks and references to Appendices
Gramont	1918 Nov 17		Cleaning up and organising	
	18		Batt. commenced march to German frontier, attacked at Lederbach in the afternoon	
Tillebeck	19		Thanksgiving Service	
"	20		Batt. moved to Cloy	
Cloy	21		General cleaning up and organising	
"	22		Battalion parade. Recreation in the afternoon	
"	23		Batt. inspection. Company commanders.	
"	24		Church Parade. Football match 1st N.R.A.M.C. Recruit NRR. 5. RWK 1	
"	25		Presentation of Decor. Ribbons by the Divisional General. Recreation in Grounds. Chonestrichs-2-0 MC. Pioneers on leave	
"	26		Battalion training under Company arrangements. Major King tournt with	
"	27		Battalion training under Company arrangements. Football in the afternoon "D"Coy v "A"Coy Bugle O	
"	28		" Football: "B"Coy 5 v "D"Coy RWK 3; Batts. killed	
"	29		Battalion Route March. Recreation in the afternoon. Batts concert in ke evening this Div. D Coy 2 v. Reg. Hdqrs. Football.	
"	30		Interior economy & General cleaning up. Major Gillard rejoined Batt. Football in afternoon "D"Coy 5 v "A"Coy Queens 0	

W. Henles Capt.
Intelligence Officer.

WAR DIARY or INTELLIGENCE SUMMARY

Army Form C. 2118.

Place	Date	Hour	Summary of Events and Information	Remarks and references to Appendices
Étroy	1918 Dec 1		Church Parade	
"	2		Battn. training under company arrangements	"A" Coy 1 v "B" Coy 0 "D" Coy 2 v "C" Coy 0 (replay) Bde Final in the afternoon
"	3		Battn. Route March — Baths	
"	4		Battn. training under company arrangements	Battn. semi-final of battn. who were in Bde to go previous days
"	5		Battn. Route March — Recreation in afternoon	Football: "D" Coy 1 v M.G.C. 0 (Bde Champ)
"	6		Battn. Parade. Football: "A" Coy 0 v R.W.K's (A Coy) 2 Semi final Bde comp.	Battn. semi-final Bde competition
"	7		Battalion training under company arrangements. Football "D" Coy v "A" Coy R.W.K's	Final Bde Comp (carried, [?] final)
"	8		Church Parade	
"	9		Battalion training under Company arrangements	Football: D Coy 3 v "A" R.W.K's 1 (Bde Comp. 1st final)
"	10		Battalion Route March	
"	11		General Cleaning up	
"	12		Battalion moved to "Blame-Capelle" (by route march)	Lt Col Smith DSO MC proceeded home
Blame Capelle	13		" " " " "Lembeg Area" (by route march)	
Lembeg Area	14		Proceeded by route march to Braine-L'Alleud Area	
"	15		Battalion Rest day for rest and general cleaning up	
"	16		Battn. proceeded by route to Bossut-Gy Area	

Army Form C. 2118.

2/3 Middlesex N.M. 32

WAR DIARY
or
INTELLIGENCE SUMMARY
(Erase heading not required.)

Instructions regarding War Diaries and Intelligence Summaries are contained in F. S. Regs., Part II. and the Staff Manual respectively. Title pages will be prepared in manuscript.

Place	Date	Hour	Summary of Events and Information	Remarks and references to Appendices
Rest Bill Area	1917 Dec 17		Battalion proceeded by route march to Longcliffe Area	
Longcliffe Area	" 18		" " " " to Hastry le Chateau	
Hastry le Chateau	" 19		" " " " to St Germain Village	
St Germain Village	" 20		" " " " to Cuflet	
Cuflet	" 21		" " " " to Latinne (Prov. of Liege)	
Latinne	" 22		Voluntary Church Service	
"	" 23		General cleaning up and organisation	
"	" 24		" of billets.	
"	" 25		Christmas Day. General holiday	
"	" 26		Inspection of billets by the Brigadier	
"	" 27		Training under Company arrangements. Afternoon devoted to Recreation	
"	" 28		" " " " "	
"	" 29		Generals inspection of billets etc	
"	" 30		" " " " "	
"	" 31		Training under Company arrangements.	

Major
for O.C. 2/3 Middx R

LONDON DIVISION
(LATE 41ST DIVISION)
123RD INFY BDE

23RD BN MIDDLESEX REGT

JAN - FEB 1919

To Intelligence Officer A8460
123 Infantry Bde.

Herewith War Diary attached
for January 1919.

(Jan - Feb)

5/2/19

T. Crawley Lieut
for OC 23rd Middx Regt.

Army Form C. 2118.

23 Fusiliers
V.01 33

WAR DIARY
or
INTELLIGENCE SUMMARY.
(Erase heading not required.)

Instructions regarding War Diaries and Intelligence Summaries are contained in F. S. Regs., Part II. and the Staff Manual respectively. Title pages will be prepared in manuscript.

Place	Date	Hour	Summary of Events and Information	Remarks and references to Appendices
Latino Jan	1919			
	1st		General cleaning up.	
	2nd		Battalion General March past the Brigadier General	
	3		Training under company arrangements; Recreation in afternoon; Boxing.	
	4		" " " " " Boxing.	
	5		Church Parade.	
	6		Battalion training under company arrangements; Recreation in the afternoon.	
	7		Route March.	
	8		Training under Company arrangements; Recreation in afternoon	
	9		" " " "	
	10		Battalion proceeded by route march to Ludenhove and entrained 16-1-18 for Bermery, arrived at Lynde 12.30 p.m.	
Lynde	11		General cleaning up & training of Details.	
	12		" " " "	
	13		Batn. training in billet; arrangements followed; making 50% of Battn. allowed to visit billeague in the afternoon.	
	14		Battn. training under Bgde arrangements; being 1 morning 5th a coming & morning of miscellaneous Batts.	
	15			
	16			

Army Form C. 2118.

WAR DIARY
INTELLIGENCE SUMMARY.
(Erase heading not required.)

Instructions regarding War Diaries and Intelligence Summaries are contained in F. S. Regs., Part II. and the Staff Manual respectively. Title pages will be prepared in manuscript.

Place	Date	Hour	Summary of Events and Information	Remarks and references to Appendices
	1919			
Lindz	May 17th		Battalion training under company arrangements during the morning	
"			Recreation in afternoon & horse exercise for mule to bullock cart drivers	
"	18th		Batt. training under company arrangements during the morning. Recreation aftern.	
"	19th		Church Parade.	
"	20th		Batt. training under company arrangements. Commenced German French & Mahratta classes for instruction. Recreation in afternoon	
"	21st		Battn. training under company arrangements	
"	22nd		" " " " " Batt. concert in evening	
"	23rd		" " " " " Batt. concert (Cross Country Run)	
"	24th		" " " " " Recreation in afternoon. Dmr E. O. Jones killed	
"	25th		Baths for Battalion; marching off Batt. to Lahore over football at Dmr E. O. Jones funeral	
"	26th		Battalion proceeded by route march to Lahore (via Trividaf—Laughny) taking over	
Lahore	27th		Church Parade.	
"	28th		Inspection of billets by C.O.	
"	29th		Training under company arrangements	
"	30th		" " " Battalion Concert.	

Army Form C. 2118.

WAR DIARY
INTELLIGENCE SUMMARY.
(Erase heading not required.)

Instructions regarding War Diaries and Intelligence Summaries are contained in F. S. Regs., Part II. and the Staff Manual respectively. Title pages will be prepared in manuscript.

Place	Date	Hour	Summary of Events and Information	Remarks and references to Appendices
Ichnat	1919 Jan 3		Battalion proceeded by route march to Colne-Kaak.	
			Malcolm Kennedy [?] Lieut Col. Commanding 29th Intelligence Regiment [?]	

WAR DIARY
or
INTELLIGENCE SUMMARY.
(Erase heading not required.)

2/3rd Middlesex Army Form C. 2118.
M 34

Place	Date	Hour	Summary of Events and Information	Remarks and references to Appendices
Cotonsted	1919 July 1		General cleaning up.	
"	2		Church service.	
"	3		Battalion parade. Practice for Presentation of Colours.	
"	4		" "	Lecture by Commander Viscount Brown "on the Bengal Army"
"	5		Inspection of billets by Divisional General.	
"	6		Battalion training under company arrangements. Baths.	"B" Coy paraded to Fort Q taking over "Y Guard" from company it relieves
"	7		Battalion parade. Practice for Presentation of Colours.	"B" Coy returns from France, the Troops kept by 4th Queens
"	8		Battalion training under company arrangements. Interior Economy inspection of billets by C.O.	
"	9		Church parade.	
"	10		Battalion parade. Practice for Presentation of Colours.	
"	11		Battalion parade to Presentation of Colours by General Sir O. Plumer. (Riviera Hotel Stadium)	Lecture on "Italy" given to Officers by The Brigadier
"	12		Battalion parade to Presentation of Colours.	by Revd Father J. Andrewetti
"	13		Battalion training under company arrangements. Guards & clerical arrangements.	
"	14		Baths.	
"	15		Battalion training under company arrangements. Football afternoon. "C" Coy v "Y Guard".	
"	16		Church Parade.	

To Intelligence Officer H/84.
123rd Infantry Bde.

Herewith War Diary and
Battalion records attached.
War Diary for February 1919.

15/3/19

[signature]
for O.C 23 Middlesex Regt.

Army Form C. 2118.

WAR DIARY
or
INTELLIGENCE SUMMARY.
(Erase heading not required.)

Place	Date	Hour	Summary of Events and Information	Remarks and references to Appendices
Cold. Kaserne	1919 Feby 17		Battalion training under Company arrangements: Inter-Battalion Cross Country race.	
"	18		"	
"	19		Two Companies Shooting on the range: Remainder Company arrangements.	
"	20		Battalion training under company arrangements. Baths.	
"	21		Interior Economy work: Inspection of billets by Brigadier.	
"	22		Two companies training & remainder Shooting on the range.	
"	23		Church Parade.	
"	24		Battalion training under Company arrangements. Festau. M&4 & 4th C.G's.O.	
"	25		Two companies training, remainder Shooting on the range.	
"	26		Battalion Parade.	
"	27		Battalion training under Company arrangements. Baths: Lieut.Col. B.A. Smith D.S.O. M.C. to Cambridge	
"	28		Battalion training under Company arrangements.	
	29			

23/3/19

[signature]
Major
Commanding 33rd Middlesex Regt.

RECORD of the 23rd. (S) Battn. MIDDLESEX REGIMENT.

The 23rd. (S) Battn. Middlesex Regiment was raised in the Autumn of 1915 by Mr. W. Joynson Hicks M.P. whose brother, Major Alfred Hicks was the first Commanding Officer. At Holmbury it received its first complement of men from the details of the 1st. Footballer's Battalion, the 17th Middlesex, and the Command was taken over by Lt. Col. W. C. C. Ash D.S.O. Thence the Battalion moved to Aldershot, where it received it's final drafts, and, after review by H.M. the King on Laffans Plain, left on the 4th May 1916, via Southampton for France. The Battalion first saw action in the front line at LE TOQUET on the 27th May, relieving the 2nd South African Battn., and remained in that area until August. On the 25th August the Battalion entrained for GORENFLOS, and after 10 days training, moved to the Somme area about FRICOURT, where the concentration of Troops was being made for the attack on the 15th September. On the 15th September the Battalion took part in the capture of FLERS, and held the front line between FLERS and GOUDECOURT against the subsequent counter attacks. During this action, the Battalion lost in Casualties 280 men and 11 Officers, including the Commanding Officer Lt. Col Ash, who subsequently died from wounds he received, the Command reverting to Major Haig Brown. After further tours in the line at GOUDECOURT and EAUCOURT L'ABBAYE, the 41st Division was withdrawn from the Somme area, and joined the 2nd Army, this Battalion taking over the line in front of the ST. ELOI Craters, where it remained for the greater part of the year 1917, taking part in the front line of assault in the Battles of MESSINES RIDGE, on June 7th, HOLLEBEKE, July 31st, and TOWER HAMLETS September 20th. After the action round HOLLEBEKE, Major A.V.A. Gayer replaced Lt. Cl Haig Brown D.S.O. as Commanding Officer, when the latter was evacuated to Hospital and to England. The Division moved at the end of September to the 4th Army Area on the Coast, where Colonel Haig Brown rejoined the Battalion. On the 14th November, the Battalion moved from this area to join the British Forces proceeding to Italy, and after a journey of 8 days by rail, detrained at WISARQUES and marched to SELVA, immediately in rear of the Montello, a distance

112 miles which was accomplished in 7 days' marching. On the 1st January 1918, a Composite Company of this Battalion undertook the first raid by British Troops over the River Piave, making the crossing with over 200 men, and with a loss of one man wounded. On the 23rd March the Battalion was recalled to France in anticipation of the coming German Offensive, and the 23rd Middlesex were in the line at BEUGNY on the 22nd. On the 23rd, 24th and 25th., the Battalion was concerned in the retirement from this position to ACHIET-LE-PETIT, where it had the great misfortune to lose it's second Commanding Officer, Colonel Haig Brown. The Battalion was in action again at COMMECOURT and BUCQUOY in this Areas, and moved on the 4th April back to the 2nd Army, and took over the front line at PASSCHENDAELE. The retirement from this position took place on the 19th April, and a new line was established at POTIJZE. While here, Lt. Col. B. A. Smith M.C. arrived to take Command from Capt. Laidlaw. After holding the line in front of YPRES for six weeks, the Battalion was withdrawn to the 2nd Army Training Area, and returned on the 2nd July to relieve the French Troops in front of Mount Kemmel, in which sector, always under threat of attack, it remained until 25th August. The 2nd 108th Battn. U.S.A. Infantry accompanied the 23rd Middlesex for one tour in the line for instruction. On the 25th August the Battalion returned to ST. OMER for two days only and was then recalled on account of the retirement of the Germans from KEMMEL. After one tour in the line at VIERSTRAAT the Battalion was moved to Reserve to train for the Attack on the 28th September. On the 29th the Battalion came to the front line of the attack at KORTEWILDE and reached the outskirts of COMINES. On the 1st October, after a flank march, the Battalion again attackd between AMERICA CORNER and GHELUWE. The next advance was on the 14 October towards COURTRAI. The LYS was crossed on the 19th, and the Battalion continued to attack and eventually crossed the SCHELDT following the retirement of the enemy on the 9th November. When the Armistice was declared on the 11th November, the Battalion was lying at NEDERBRAKEL.

Casualties suffered by the 23rd Middlesex Regiment are as follows:-

	Officers	O. R's
Killed	17	301
Wounded	48	1091
Missing	1	213
Died of Wounds	2	89
Total Casualties.	68	1694

HONOURS and AWARDS gained by Officers and men of the 23rd MIDDLESEX REGIMENT since proceeding overseas on the 3rd. May 1916.

Distinguished Service Order.	4
Military Cross.	18
Bar to Military Cross.	1
Distinguished Conduct Medal.	8
Military Medal.	89
Bar to Military Medal.	3
Meritorious Service Medal.	8
French Croix de Guerre.	4
Belgian " " "	7
Italian Bronze Medal for Valour.	1
Mentioned in Despatches.	15
Total Distinctions.	156